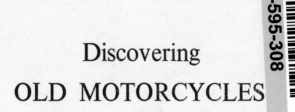

Discovering
OLD MOTORCYCLES

T. E. Crowley

Shire Publications Ltd.

CONTENTS

ACKNOWLEDGEMENTS

Photographs are acknowledged as follows: Crown Copyright, Science Museum, London, plates 2, 6, 9, 32; Science Museum, London, and Humber Ltd., plate 4; Science Museum, London, and Triumph Engineering Co. Ltd., plate 5; *Motor Cycle*, London, plates 23, 24, cover; British Photo Engraving Co. and *Motor Cycle*, London, plates 26, 27; Copyright National Motor Museum, Beaulieu, plate 10; Shuttleworth Collection, plate 3; C. E. Allen, plate 19; J. Boulton, plates 7, 8, 13, 14; A. Marfell, plates 15, 20; J. Masterman, plates 28; C. and S. Thomas, plates 1, 11, 16, 17, 30, 31; A. L. G. Wallis, plates 21, 25, 29. The cover design by Robin Ollington shows a touring Quadrant of 1906, still clearly showing its bicycle ancestry. A single lever controlled ignition switch, decompressor and throttle. A spring fork is fitted but the automatic inlet has not yet been abandoned.

1. WHY OLD MOTORCYCLES?

One man's collection is another's load of rubbish, and for those without the acquisitive urge, it is a difficult thing to understand why anyone should want to amass a quantity of useless objects, even valuable ones such as glass paperweights or cast-iron doorstops. Few things can be less interesting to many people than the rusty remains of a defunct motorcycle, but for others it can pose a fascinating problem of restoration, and the hours spent bringing it back to life and restoring its livery may be among the happiest and most absorbing of one's leisure time; furthermore, the result is useful as well as ornamental! Veteran cars, of course, have become quite a part of the social scene; they may be seen, professionally res- tored, in the spacious showrooms of main agents or at society weddings. Motor rallies, well publicised, are attended by shining antiques piloted by notable people some of whom have little inclination to roll up their sleeves and assist in the difficult task of persuading the old engine to go; dealers spring up and prices rise accordingly, and pictures of the famous models of yesteryear are to be seen adorning table- mats, beer glasses, ashtrays and wallpaper.

The world of old motorcycles has a rather different appear- ance. It is an introspective world which seems to keep its activities rather much to itself, and troubles little whether the general public knows about it or not. Groups of enthu- siasts gather and become absorbed in fascinating technicali- ties, exchange precious bits of engine, recount stories of discovery or disappointment, and prepare their machines for rally or concours. The outside world passes them by.

This introspection is a pity, but it does have its advantages. It mostly stems from the time when the motorcycle ceased to be an essential part of the education of most healthy young men. The pressure of four-wheeled motoring with its exploited appeal to comfort and convenience pushed motorcycling activities into a corner, manufacturers lost many of their best designers to more profitable fields and ceased to advertise in the national press, and a self-perpetuating state of things set in where motorcycles were thought of as ridden only by people with unusual and probably reprehensible tastes. The game had ceased to be part of the British way of life and the public conceived the average motorcyclist as an adolescent who had grown out of his toy trains and had enough money to buy a glittering and noisy monster equipped with dangerous-looking gadgets apparently designed to hinder proper control, and on which contraption he proceeded to make a nuisance of himself.

The impression is a natural one and it is a tragedy that the worst aspect of the game is the most obtrusive—almost the only one by which the public makes its judgements. There is, however, much more to the hobby of motorcycles than this, and the vintage movement is one of its most interesting facets.

In comparing the machines available today with those on the market twenty or more years ago, differences can be seen not only of degree but of kind as well. At least half the pleasure of owning a motorbike is in working on it and improving its capabilities. It was said by the late Robertson Scott, founder of the *Countryman*, that the motorcycle is the greatest single aid to education, and he must have been thinking not only of getting to know one's country, and perhaps foreign parts as well, but of developing the skill and resource to put things right when they go wrong and to understand the work of the men who designed and built the machine. The proper way to learn the game is certainly on an old and neglected specimen. Every involuntary stop teaches a lesson in ingenuity and every maintenance period is an opportunity for improvement; after a year or two a great store of skill and knowledge has been built up. With it comes an affection for the game and probably for the particular machine as well. Much of all this is denied to the young man who buys a modern machine with its complete reliability, its lack of individual character, and its demands to be returned to the dealer for a replacement unit when anything goes wrong.

So, perhaps, one reason for the interest in old motorbikes may be said to emerge. One can exercise ingenuity on them and they are responsive to one's efforts. There is, and always has been, a type of man who would do anything short of selling his soul in the service of machinery. It is not just any kind of machine that enslaves these men; they will have nothing to do with diesel engines for instance, or electric motors. The machine has to be one which requires constant skilled attention to keep it functioning at its best. Read 'McAndrew's Hymn' by Kipling, who understood the breed; it is about the devotion of the old ship's engineer to his engines, the triple-expansion steam engines which he had tended many times round the world until their beat was the beat of his own heart. The massive Cornish beam pumps of the eighteenth century and the condensing engines which followed them needed an incredible amount of skill to keep them going with anything like efficiency, and they always got it. When the train driver was responsible for his own locomotive, nobody else dared to touch it. In everything which concerned it he was

4

absolute dictator, and its spotless finish indicated not only a loving care, but a matchless skill and determination to get out of it the very best that the engine was capable of.

Modern machinery by its very nature is quite unfitted to satisfy the instincts of such people, and all that is left to most of them is to polish up some mass-produced little car on a Saturday morning. Others, however, have turned to older machinery in its various forms, and set themselves the task of restoring it to its original efficiency, partly for the immense satisfaction they get from it, but also as a tribute to the mighty men of old who constructed and worked the things by the cunning of their practical knowledge and the sweat of their brows, and without so much that we now take for granted. Such machinery consists not merely of old vehicles, but anything from complete railway systems, windmills and paddle steamers to muskets and verge watches. Things which a few years ago were obsolete and mostly paid the penalty, are now treasured for the potential in them. Machines even now being scrapped will be bitterly regretted in a few years time, as people realise more and more the treasure that lies in tangible history.

For anyone interested in industrial archaeology, the motorcycle as a study subject has many advantages. The range of designs is considerable and varied, it covers sixty or seventy years, and the individual machines available to see and study run into thousands, both in museums and at vintage meetings, where interested strangers are always welcome and find themselves absorbed in historical and technical details in no time. A motorcycle takes up comparatively little room, and neither oldish machines nor spare parts need cost a lot of money. The dealers have not as yet moved in very greatly, and most bargains are driven privately. As long as the moneymakers remain a small minority, so will the interest remain a friendly one in which even a rather impecunious youngster may take part.

For let it here be understood that this is not merely an old man's game. It is true that we still have with us many who rode, and a few who became famous, in the golden era of the twenties, riders who have never lost the fascination of the two-wheeled game and still forgather whenever they can. Their achievements are not forgotten and their advice is invaluable; but vintage motorcycles are also the chosen study of growing numbers of young men and women who find in them something different from the monotony of modern vehicles, and a satisfaction in proving their skill at maintaining and riding something beyond the capabilities of the average motorist.

2. HOW OLD MOTORCYCLES MAY BE DISCOVERED

A veteran machine is defined as one manufactured before the end of 1914. The date forms a good historical break because very few machines were made for civilian use during the Great War. A vintage motorcycle must have been built between 1915 and the end of 1930. The choice of date here is perhaps both more subtle and more arbitrary, but it is based on the idea that before this latter date things were in the main hand-built by trained craftsmen, and after it mass-produced methods became general and many factors of excellent quality became lost or outdated. Obviously, such a thing did not happen overnight, but 1930 was the year of the great slump, when many famous and historical manufacturers closed their doors for the last time, others turned to producing very cheap (and sometimes nasty) models in an effort to keep going, and most of the larger factories saw the need for steps towards rationalised production.

It is not true, as some diehards will have it, that no good motorcycles were manufactured after 1930. There were bad products before then, just as there were some firms known for hand-finishing their products for years afterwards: for example Brough Superior, Levis, Scott and Velocette. Most of the industry's output however, became mass-produced, with all the advantages and disadvantages that that implies.

Motorcycles manufactured between 1930 and 1945 are known as 'post-vintage', and many of them are of considerable interest. Advanced designs continued to be offered to the public, though few of them proved to be commercial successes; the conservatism of the average rider seemed on the increase, and not everything which was demanded by the pundits was bought when it became available. Single-cylinder design was raised to a noteworthy pitch of efficiency.

Anything later than 1945 is called 'post-war', and many items are decidedly worth preserving. Some manufacturers foresaw a new future for a new type of motorcycle, and were enterprising enough in the earlier part of the era to scrap their pre-war designs and start afresh in an effort to provide the public not merely with more speed, but with greater refinement of performance, better brakes and steering, and a cleaner and more comfortable ride, all from first principles rather than by detail improvement of what were becoming old-fashioned designs.

At this point it might be as well to try to define the difference between motorcycle and motor-car. This seems a matter of no difficulty these days, but it was not always so, and many of the early designs partook of the characteristics of both. By legislation, since the 1930s, a motorcycle is a vehicle with less than four wheels and weighing under eight hundredweight, and this includes most of the well-known three-wheelers such as the Morgan, BSA and Raleigh. In Victorian times and after, a motor-car is surely a vehicle possessing coachwork and usually doors, while a motorcycle is one with a saddle (although some had padded seats and arm-rests) and handlebars. Of three-wheelers, models such as the 1895 Benz were certainly cars and others such as the Leon Bollée, where one sat in an open frame, just as certainly motorcycles. If a tricycle was fitted with an engine and steered by a wheel, or if two bicycles were clamped together side by side with a saddle and handlebars between them, the result was a motorcycle, even though such specimens are usually admitted to motor-car rallies.

There are two ways of discovering old motorcycles; one, as with Norman castles, is to read about them, go where they may be found, and study them in detail. The other, as with postage stamps, is to amass your own collection. This demands suitable storage space and a certain amount of cash. If your ambition is to acquire, you must decide whether to look for something which has been in a hedge bottom for years, something which, though worn, is in some kind of running order, or something which has already been restored to its pristine brilliance, and may cost a good deal.

There are many examples about of machines restored to smartness and efficiency from little more than a twisted mass of rusty metal, but to do this needs patience and not a little skill. In other words, if there are items in the project you cannot tackle yourself, you must be able to find someone else who can—and will, and this is important, because helping somebody with heavy restoration work is usually rather un-profitable if it is done in the line of business. It is perhaps better to start with a machine which is substantially complete and more or less capable of running, but once you have made up your mind to own an old motorcycle, the Fates are in-clined to take over and you find yourself picking up whatever you can. The search for machines lying forgotten in barns or under workbenches goes on all the time and they do still turn up, but thirty years is a long time for an old machine to lie undisturbed, and even this, when found, would probably not be vintage. The days when someone might find a Holden or a Werner, forgotten since the days of Edward VII, are surely now over.

The best way of finding out how to get things done or where to get obsolete parts is by joining a club. Of these, the Vintage Motor Cycle Club exists to help and inform everybody interested in old motorcycles everywhere. It is organised on a regional basis and contact with the local section will bring help and friendly advice. Probably too, if you want it that way, somebody has an old machine that he may sell you for a reasonable sum. Machines and parts are advertised in the monthly *Bulletin*. If you live in London, join the Collectors' Club and share its friendly meetings. Perhaps a one-make club exists for the machines which interest you, and if it does, you should not fail to join it. Such clubs have registers of engine and frame numbers which are of considerable value, and it is a courtesy to provide any details you can find to supplement their records; also, they have helpful spares secretaries.

If you are not already skilled in mechanics but wish to become so, the stripping down and restoration of an old motorbike is certainly one of the best possible ways to learn. Your first machine under such circumstances should be not too old and not too complex. A well-worn post-vintage two-stroke would often be ideal; this is possibly something you may feel inclined to look down on, but you will find it can set you plenty of problems before you have succeeded in restoring it to anything like good order. Even practice in laying on a neat coat of enamel is obtained just as well on a cheap relic as on a valuable antique. If you were to come across something like a veteran four-cylinder FN, treasure it but do no work on it until you have gained a lot of experience, because such exotic machinery was cunningly built on lines not since used by any other designer, and even most of the screw threads are left-handed! In other words, you need practice and experience not to do considerable damage by your efforts, and remember that it will cost you in the order of £100 to get a cylinder made for *this* model.

It may occur to you at this point that the finances of the game are complex, and to some extent this is so, although it does not mean that you have to spend a lot of money to get pleasure out of the hobby. Veterans are few and undoubtedly expensive, but an average late-vintage machine in fair order may cost you little more than the price of a set of golf clubs, or shall we say, two or three times what it cost when new. Some people tire of their restoration work before it is finished, and you may be offered a box of bits instead of a bike. Beware of this, for such machines are rarely complete even when the owners think they are, and you will be wise to reckon on the absence of one or two important pieces. Such boxfuls should come cheap unless the work done to date is obviously of excellent quality.

If private researches lead you to an old machine in a barn, you are lucky, but beware of the owner who responds to your interest by suddenly deciding he has something of great value, because very often he has not. You may possibly have come across, shall we say, a 1938 350c.c. BSA with an engine that will not turn over, a missing tank and exhaust, and of course fairly rusty. Such a find would be dear at £5. It is not vintage, there is nothing of particular interest about its design, to restore it to good order will certainly cost a lot more than it will be worth when done, and only a few parts are likely to be useable as spares for other machines.

Do not, however, be put off acquiring an interesting machine merely because it is incomplete; remember that even quite unusual replacement parts can normally be obtained in the end, given time, patience and a few contacts, and if you yourself have a few parts for other peoples' models, so much the better.

---

3. DATING AND RESTORATION

The problem of dating an old machine can be a thorny one but it is of some importance to determine the point. It is a great help if the log book, which will give the date of original registration, is available, and one should then check the engine, frame and registration numbers. Normally little further verification should be necessary, although there are many instances of numbers being incorrectly listed in log books and of registration numbers being switched, or even allotted to two vehicles at the same time.

If the machine is without benefit of documents but has readable number plates, it is worth writing to the original registration authority; many of them are helpful and will provide the original date of application. The Vintage Motor Cycle Club issues a detailed listing of its members' machines, and picking out those with similar numbers can provide good clues.

The date of registration however, does not always give a reliable indication of the date of manufacture; a machine may spend a long time in store before being sold. Motorcycles used by the services are not registered until they are sold off second-hand, which may be years after manufacture, and foreign machines are naturally registered only when they enter the country, perhaps after long periods of use overseas.

The marque specialist (VMCC scheme) for your machine can advise you on receipt of full particulars, especially engine and frame numbers; after that it is largely a case of studying such catalogues, articles and advice as you can get.

The age of a motorcycle is generally regarded as that of its frame, this being the item least likely to be renewed during use. Many models throughout the years were fitted with proprietary engines and these may well have been made earlier or later than the frame to which they are fitted, but if the difference proves to be more than a year or two, you probably have a rebuilt model, something of a mongrel, and the date ceases to matter very much. You cannot insist that you have a veteran merely because the frame was made before 1915; this is a matter which concerns the majority of the parts, not merely a few of them. It is of course, almost certain that previous owners fitted replacement parts through the years, and many of these parts may be incongruous; there may have been mistaken ideas of modernisation (flat-tank Sunbeams have been seen fitted with dual seats), and an amateur rebuilder can create not only a mess but a mystery as well for the would-be restorer into whose hands the machine may fall twenty or thirty years later. One comfort is that whatever the model there is sure to be an expert in that particular make, there are means of finding him, and there is a likelihood that he will agree to give expert advice.

Let us assume that the enthusiast has decided to restore a certain machine, and has studied it sufficiently to have a good idea of how much of it is original and how much consists of later additions or replacements; no doubt there will be bits missing as well. The decision on restoration then depends on several factors.

First of all, does the restorer wish to possess a machine as nearly as possible in its original condition or does he feel inclined to make a 'concours' model out of it? Paradoxically, if an old machine is not good enough for the first alternative it is better to turn it into a concours specimen because in the latter case many of the fittings and some of the main items can be replacements or fabrications so long as they are exactly in keeping with the make and year. Motorcycles in original condition are not common because they must never, during the time of their existence, have passed through a period of gross neglect—which is the common lot of everything obsolescent. Even with good treatment over the years plating will deteriorate, particularly as manufacturing techniques were comparatively primitive in those days, and you may feel that the restoration work will look decidedly unfinished unless the bright parts are replated. Go ahead, but remember your finish will then be a replacement one and not the original. Once a frame has been rubbed down and repainted, the original finish has gone for ever, so the kind of paint you use for refinishing does not matter, although the colour may well do so. Similarly, unless you are entering concours competitions, you can please yourself about the plating, remembering that chromium is the longest lasting! Avoid using aluminium paint as a substitute, however.

The resources and money needed to render a machine in concours condition are considerable, for your final product must appear just as it left the factory; in fact many enthusiasts go beyond this point and work up a lustrous finish such as no factory would ever have been able to provide, except at a loss. Even a cadmium-plated bolthead is likely to disqualify you. At most meetings the entry will have to prove itself by completing a scheduled run, so the handsome must 'do' as well as 'be', and this is as it should be, since motorcycles are restored to ride rather than to put in glass cases.

To restore some ancient specimens may possibly need the resources of a local foundry, forge or machine-shop, and this is all right if you are prepared to pay for the results. Almost anything in metal can be duplicated locally, but remember that no tyre can be made outside a tyre factory, and some types and sizes of tyre are now unobtainable—in fact the moulds have been destroyed. This is a matter to consider in obtaining an old machine; there is an excellent tyre scheme run through the VMCC, so that definite information is available about this vexed subject. If no tyres exist of the size hoped for, the wheels will have to be rebuilt with new rims to take an alternative.

There are other pitfalls for the beginner; for instance, some frames and forks in the early days were very lightly built, barely up to their work even when new, and the combined effects of corrosion and metal fatigue may render them dangerous. For similar reasons it is unwise to over-improve the usually poor brakes on an old machine, even if such a thing is found possible, because of the extra load so thrown on the forks, frame and spokes. You just have not got modern efficiency and your only remedy is to adjust your driving methods accordingly.

A lot of time will probably need to be spent removing crankiness even when the restoration might be thought complete. The first run usually produces a number of surprises, and further adjustments are needed. You may well find that your carburettor and ignition settings vary considerably from anything in the textbooks, and you had better arm yourself with a handful of sparking plugs of various types, some engines in their old age being more particular than others. Beware also of the divers effects of rust in the tank (where it is often undetected), of someone having drilled out a carburettor jet so that you have not got what you think you have, and of mysterious ignition troubles resulting from half-melted shellac in the magneto. Certain it is that if you can arrange to provide a strong spark at the right time, the majority of your troubles are usually over—more failures and poor performances are the result of ignition than of all other causes put together.

It is a curious fact that most really old motorcycles can be persuaded to run much more effectively than they did when new; this is the result of using modern lubricating oil, tyres, plugs, batteries and so on.

A few words are perhaps needed about storage. When your precious machine has reached a stage which satisfies you, it will in the nature of things immediately start to deteriorate once more. The only real answer is heated storage, not available to most of us, but if your painting work has been laid on a well rust-primed foundation according to the textbooks, and your metal parts well greased for winter conditions, dust-sheets and 'Banrust' paper should keep the machine in reasonably good order when out of use. To paraphrase a proverb, the best preservative is the owner's eye. Good motorcycles of past years are increasing in value and interest, and it is worth while to take a little trouble.

4. THE PIONEERS 1884-1900

Very little is usually known about the early days of large industries. Few of the pioneers bothered to record their own efforts; in fact they were more concerned to hide them from the world and their possible rivals until a measure of success had been achieved and financial returns seemed possible. All this is certainly so in the case of motor vehicles; the records are fragmentary, and it seems likely that many early designs were lost or destroyed. The real ancestors of the motorcycle were perhaps the steam tricycles which were made from the eighteenth century onwards; many of them undoubtedly ran, but as they were not usually permitted the use of public roads, the incentive to build them must have been largely academic.

The problem of applying the internal combustion engine to road vehicles was tackled independently by several engineers in the mid 1880s. N. A. Otto had laid down the principle of the four-stroke cycle in 1876 and Clerk did the same for the two-stroke pumping-type engine in 1881. Both methods were tried in the very early engines, but the enormous difficulties in making a workable mechanism out of a mere principle can be understood when one reads, for instance, of the experiments which were carried out with gunpowder as the propelling agent. Many of the early workers undoubtedly followed impracticable ideas, but few of those whose names we know failed to add some contribution to progress.

We must remember, too, that in the 1880s even the bicycle as we know it did not exist—a two-wheeler was almost necessarily a penny-farthing, and what was known as the 'safety' bicycle, invented by Starley, did not become popular until the early nineties. For this and other reasons such as the weight of the engine, the first motorcycles all had more than two wheels.

It seems possible that the first motorcycle successfully built and run was produced by an Englishman, Edward Butler, of Erith. His design dates from 1884, and the machine was certainly in running order in 1886 or 1887. It was a tricycle with a steering pair of front wheels, one each side of the driver's seat, and a single wheel behind flanked by two cylinders which faced forward with piston rods working on crossheads and long, curved connecting rods transmitting the power from there to the live axle of the rear wheel through a chain drive and a six-to-one reduction gear. The cylinders were water-cooled and, unlike any other design for years afterwards, Butler employed a float-feed carburettor and electric ignition. Things like these seem to us now an essential part of all petrol engines, and it is strange how long some of the pioneers struggled with unpractical alternatives.

Butler's machine was not developed any further, since there was remarkably little encouragement for motor vehicles in this country—in fact they were restricted by law to 4 m.p.h., although it is not true that a red flag was ever carried in front of a motor vehicle. Continental soil was more fertile at this time, however, and Gottlieb Daimler, usually thought of as the father of the motor industry, produced his first machine in 1885. This was a primitive hobby-horse type of bicycle with wooden wheels, with the engine mounted vertically in the frame and two small outrigger wheels to ensure that the arrangement remained approximately vertical. It was intended more as a mobile test-bed than as a road-going concern, but the engine showed considerable promise and a two-cylinder version was built before the inventor turned his attention to cars. The engines possessed an aluminium crankcase containing a connecting rod working between two flywheels in the modern fashion, air cooling and a primitive form of poppet valve.

One or two other inventors produced motor tricycles with a single front wheel, notably Carl Benz of Mannheim, but these were generally coachbuilt and partook more of the nature of cars than motorcycles. J. D. Rootes, however, built a motor tricycle with saddle and handlebars in 1892, and his general layout was followed by most of the subsequent designers. His water-cooled engine was inverted behind the rear axle—a two-stroke unit using vaporised oil and driving via reduction bevels. It seems to have been a practical layout, although details of its performance are not on record.

The year 1895 brought some important advances; in France the Marquis de Dion modified Daimler's engine and installed it behind the rear axle of a pedalling tricycle. The engine was now quite a practical proposition and the machine proved a commercial success, being marketed up to about 1902, not only by de Dion but by many licensees and imitators (plate 1), and was developing all the time.

A German motor bicycle appeared in 1895 under the name of Hildebrand and Wolfmuller, and a number were sold to the public, one being imported into this country for demonstration purposes, finally ending up in the Science Museum. They had open duplex frames; the two water-cooled cylinders were horizontal, open-ended, and driving the rear wheel by directly coupled cranks. The firm's trade mark was a little angel. A somewhat similar layout was designed by Colonel H. Capel Holden in the same year, but his cylinders faced each other in two pairs, with a crosshead and long cranks to the rear axle, the rear wheel being made very small for 'gearing down' purposes. This has claims to being the first four-cylinder motorcycle, and arrangements were made to produce it commercially. It came on the market in 1899, beautifully made and finished but already out-dated by new developments, and not many were sold.

In 1895, too, an American, E. J. Pennington, built at Coventry a bicycle and a tandem, both fitted with two-cylinder engines projecting behind the rear wheel and driving it by direct-coupled cranks. The cylinders had no cooling arrangements; carburation was merely a petrol drip into the intake tube, ignition by battery and coil with a wiper contact on the piston heads. The layout was not practical, although the machines were persuaded to go for short distances for demonstration purposes and were supposed to have attained 30 m.p.h. The silver-tongued American returned to the States £100,000 richer, but no further examples were ever built.

The pedal cycle was now well established; it had tangent-spoked wheels, pneumatic tyres and driving chains, all items useful to ease the path of the motorcycle designer. Open cranks and exposed pistons in those days of dusty roads and deep muddy ruts must have reduced the life of the engines to a few hundred miles, even if they could be persuaded to go as far as that; no more were built after the Holden, all subsequent machines having enclosed crankcases. Surface carburation was, however, universal up to the turn of the century —a method by which air was drawn through the petrol tank by the engine, vaporisation being assisted by the exhaust pipe passing through the tank. The air/vapour mixture needed continual adjustment according to weather and road surface, and speed changes were usually effected by advancing and retarding the ignition, where this was electric. Often, however, it consisted of a dangerous contraption involving a platinum tube kept hot by a small petrol burner which fired the gas in the cylinder by pre-ignition, and usually set fire to the machine whenever there was a skid.

The Beeston motor tricycle appeared in 1897, very much along de Dion lines, and attained popularity. The firm also made quadricycles, an arrangement based on a cycle frame with four wheels, an engine behind and a basket seat or padded chair for a passenger between the front wheels. Some of these machines were even exported. Another tricycle, the Bollée, well designed with a low-slung chassis, front passenger seat and single-cylinder engine alongside the rear wheel, earned quite a name for speed and reliability, aided as it was by a three-speed sliding gear much in advance of its day. This was to have been made under licence by Humber, but a fire destroyed their factory about this time, so a separate firm, the British Motor Syndicate, was organised to produce a number of variants. Humber themselves had been building a 'tricar', a cycle with two front wheels, a passenger seat between them, and an engine mounted behind the rear wheel. This they called the 'Olympia Tandem' and exhibited it at the 1899 show, although sales were few.

The motor tricycle industry was well under way and a number of famous firms were producing variations of the de Dion layout, notably the MMC (used in the Boer War), the Enfield, with de Dion engine, the Dennis, Swift, Riley, Star, and the Ariel, which moved the engine forward of the rear axle, thus greatly improving the weight distribution.

Two-wheelers were at a discount, and the only one made in any quantity, the Werner, had a particularly bad reputation for sideslip. This is hardly surprising when it is realised that the engine was mounted above the front wheel and was fitted with hot-tube ignition. The model was first put on the market in 1897 in France, and it was made under licence in Coventry, with coil and battery ignition, in 1899. Several good examples remain (plate 2). One more advanced design appeared before the end of the century; this was a motor-wheel designed by Perks and Birch and later taken over and produced by Singer (plate 3). The engine was enclosed in two spoked aluminium plates forming the driving wheel; it was fitted with a surface carburettor and with a low-tension magneto—probably the first design to be so equipped. The unit was compact and well thought out, and could be fitted to any bicycle or tricycle, but its cog-wheel drive made it harsh in power delivery, and it had very little power anyway.

5.   EARLY DEVELOPMENT 1900-1914

The last chapter dealt with the origins of the motorcycle in some detail, and although few who read this will ever have a chance of owning a nineteenth-century example, it is right that the struggles of the first pioneers should be recorded. These men, in the days when even metallurgy was in its infancy, attempted to translate half-understood theory into practice without the benefit of written manuals, training, experience or any of the aids to design which might today be thought absolutely essential. They had only their own craftsman's instinct to guide them, and the progress they made was remarkable, especially in the face of the violent and unreasonable prejudice to which they were exposed. As a result of their efforts, the new century ushered in a period of prosperity, when the motorcycle with two, three or four wheels became available in quantity and variety, and offered the purchaser some degree of reliability. Stops by the wayside continued, of course, with some frequency, but in the majority of occasions they concerned something which the ingenious could remedy on the spot. Each increase in engine efficiency showed up weaknesses in forks, frames, spokes and transmission, and every motorcyclist was an expert puncturemender: horse and hob nails abounded and tyres were very thin. Ignition parts were mostly made out of what has been described as a form of metallic putty, the life of plugs and valves was short, and most people carried plenty of engine spares—and often a whip for hostile dogs. Motoring life was certainly still an adventure into the unknown, but it was possible for an ordinary tourist to cover big mileages with success.

The years 1899–1901 saw the beginnings of quite a number of firms whose names were to become famous in the industry for all time. The earlier year saw the beginning of experiments with Werner-type engines designed to clip to ordinary cycles. Machines along these lines were produced by the brothers Harry and Charles Collier (both later destined to win the TT), and by Alfred A. Scott; these activities led within a few years to the founding of the Matchless and Scott factories respectively. Joah Phelon in 1900 took out patents for a very neat engine arrangement with inclined cylinder taking the place of the front portion of the frame and a chain drive to the rear wheel; this design led to the foundation of the Phelon and Moore factory at Cleckheaton, and machines of basically similar layout were built under the Panther trade name as late as 1963. The design was adopted and produced by Humber under licence for both bicycles and tricycles (plate 4).

The Raleigh and Enfield concerns both manufactured variants of the Werner design in 1900, the latter having a long twisted rawhide belt driving the rear wheel. Belt drive was certainly the answer to the harsh transmission of the earlier machines, but brought with it troubles such as unreliability, and slippage in wet weather.

The two-wheeler was gaining ground, however, and a great step forward was taken when the Minerva engine became available. This was designed in 1899 by two Swiss engineers, and produced in Belgium; of 211c.c. capacity, it was provided with attachments to clip to the front down tube of any bicycle and thus made it possible for almost any cycle shop to become a motorcycle factory. Scores of them did; the first substantial firm in this country to adopt it on a large scale seems to have been Bayliss-Thomas, late in 1900, under the Excelsior trademark, and they were followed by Alldays, Enfield, Ivel, Phoenix, Coventry-Progress, Quadrant and Triumph, all in 1901. This year too saw the founding of the Indian concern in the USA, and of AJS, when the Stevens brothers marketed a machine powered by a small American engine called the Mitchell. Other firms of note to launch into motorcycle production about the same time included Imperial Cycles (later New Imperial) with an all-British machine powered by a 500c.c. engine and direct belt drive, and OEC, a racing 4 h.p. design by F. J. Osborne, built in Coventry.

The Minerva engine underwent continuous improvement, and by 1903 both valves were mechanically operated by cams situated in the crankcase. The old automatic inlet valve, opened by the suction of the engine and closed again by a weak and very sensitive spring, had the big disadvantage of power loss at low revolutions (plate 5); nevertheless, there was a surprising amount of opposition to positive operation of the valve on the grounds of 'complication', and the old type lingered on until the First World War.

17

1902 brought designs by W. Hillman of Coventry and William Morris of Oxford, also the Rex, which won a great reputation as a speedster, the Hobart and the Coventry-Eagle. Alfred Scott started production of a two-stroke engine-assisted bicycle strikingly unlike his later machines. On the whole, manufacturers were very reluctant to design special frames, the 'clip-on' type of motor was very much the order of the day, and even this was not expected to do more than assist the exertions of the cyclist. Now, however, Werner came out with a completely new design, having a frame built to hold the engine vertically low down in what afterwards became the conventional position. The machine had power and reliability and won most of the competitions for which it entered; its effect on future design was profound and its merits were speedily evident to many British engineers. Although the Werner layout was well protected by patents, these were circumvented by various forms of loop or cradle frame, and before the end of the year vertical engines mounted inside the frame were available from many factories including Clarendon, James, Quadrant, Bradbury, Rex, New Hudson and Phoenix, while on the Continent, Peugeot, FN and NSU followed the same trend. James Norton, chainmaker, used the Clement engine in a machine he offered under the name 'Energette'. Various British factories produced proprietary engines, the most important of which was the JAP, fitted by Triumph in 1903, and this year also brought the first commercial sprung rear frame, marketed by BAT, the Rover motorcycle, and the first sidecars in a variety of tentative designs mostly based on leather-backed or wickerwork armchairs with footwells (plate 13). They speedily ousted the two-wheel armchair trailer which had been hitched on behind the saddle and had proved the most uncomfortable and dangerous form of passenger transport known.

Number plates became compulsory in 1904; the speed limit was raised to 20 m.p.h., and good spray carburettors and high-voltage magnetos came on the market in quantity. Bowden wire controls were introduced and front forks were strutted for strength; one or two makers such as Quadrant even fitted a crude form of sprung fork. The rubber and canvas V-section belt began to replace the twisted rawhide drive (as fitted to treadle sewing machines) and JAP put on the market an engine of overhead valve design. 60 m.p.h. was attained on racing tracks. Altogether, the motorcycle was gaining strength and constructively measuring up to its problems, but it was just at this time that a big recession set in. The flow of new designs slowed down as sales dropped, even though 1905 saw the flat twin design by Joseph Barter (later to

18

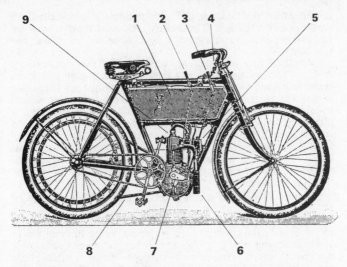

A new-type design of 1903, when the industry realised that the place for an engine was in the frame: The Star with French Griffon engine, sold for £60

1. Sheet-metal box containing petrol and oil tanks, coil and battery
2. Throttle lever
3. Ignition advance lever
4. Ignition switch
5. Spray carburettor
6. Silencer
7. Contact breaker
8. Direct-belt drive from engine pulley
9. Automatic inlet valve

become the Douglas), a side-by-side vertical twin by Berclay, and the first four-cylinder FN. Many firms vanished overnight and it became evident that a large proportion of designs were underdeveloped and unfit for marketing. It seemed that only Triumphs, under their extremely able director J. M. Schulte, were able to maintain their sales. Phelon and Moore, however, were leading the way in design by introducing a trouble-free two-speed gear involving two chain drives to a countershaft fitted with a selective clutch (a layout later to be adopted by A. A. Scott), and by boldly omitting the pedalling gear. V-twin engines were now on the market (plate 9).

Interest returned in 1907 with the establishment of the TT races in the Isle of Man, and the building of the Brooklands track. Designers had previously attempted to win races by fitting larger and larger engines into lighter and lighter frames, but the new facilities for racing showed the fallacy of such ideas and proved ideal testing grounds. They aroused considerable public interest and ruthlessly pinpointed all weaknesses of design. The benefit to the industry was incalculable, and the motorcycle rapidly gained in speed and reliability.

In 1908 Scott marketed his water-cooled two-stroke twin, built by Jowetts and equipped with two-speed gear and kick-start; it caused a sensation and speedily gained its long-lived reputation in competition work. Another outstanding design to appear was Barnes's Zenith Gradua, which provided a change of gear by opening and closing the pulley flanges on the direct-belt drive and simultaneously sliding the rear wheel in and out to maintain belt tension. The system was successful enough to be barred from hill-climbing competitions as 'unfair', a fact of which the manufacturer took full advantage in his advertisements.

Chater-Lea entered the market in 1909 with a V-twin of excellent quality, and from 1910 the trade recovered steadily, and design improvements came in a steady flow. The need for a 'free-engine clutch' was beginning to be understood in the thickening traffic, and a number of two-speed gears appeared, notably on a well-designed Royal Enfield light twin with Vickers engine. Veloce reappeared with a workaday sidevalve model and Lea Francis designed a luxurious machine with a countershaft gearbox mounted behind the engine in what later became the orthodox position, fully enclosed chain drive and a V-twin engine from JAP (plate 12), thus forestalling by two years the almost incomparable Sunbeam, with its enamel almost as hard as steel, designed along similar lines. Other new firms that year included Clyno, Omega, and the four-cylinder Wilkinson with a bucket seat (plate 8). A number of rotary-valve engines were tried out on the public with limited success; the best of them was the Corah. Rudge-Whitworth and BSA joined the ranks of the larger manufacturers, DOT produced a dropped frame with low saddle position, and PV a good rear-sprung frame. Two-stroke lightweights began to appear, the Levis of 1911 being the first popular example (plate 7); three-speed hub gears, stronger versions of those on contemporary bicycles, also became available from Armstrong and Sturmey-Archer. They were remarkably compact and ingenious pieces of mechanism, excellent when expertly maintained but tricky to adjust and liable to destroy themselves if not looked after. In the same year Rudge produced their famous 'Multi' gear, with fifteen notches on the gearchange, operating on movable pulley flanges on both engine shaft and rear wheel, allowing the engine to slow down as the machine gathered speed very smoothly, and it became deservedly popular (plate 14).

Both Villiers and Blackburne offered proprietary engines in 1913, many of the larger manufacturers revised and extended their ranges, and new names included the Ivy, Hazlewood and Royal Ruby. The fashion for 1914 seemed to be for larger engines, the Rudge Multi going to 750c.c. and the Excelsior even to 800c.c. in one cylinder. New V- and flat twins became available, notably designs by W. E. Brough, W. A. Weaver (Montgomery) and Granville Bradshaw (the first ABC). Two-stroke lightweights proliferated, notably from Clyno, Connaught, Levis, Radco, and Velocette, and also Triumph (plate 18), who fitted a two-speed countershaft gearbox. Starting these machines was very easy, and some of them dared to dispense with pedals. The new Calthorpe lightweight and the JES motorised bicycle both had small four-stroke engines.

This brings us very briefly to the end of the veteran era and the outbreak of war. Civilian machines continued to be available for the time being but in reduced numbers.

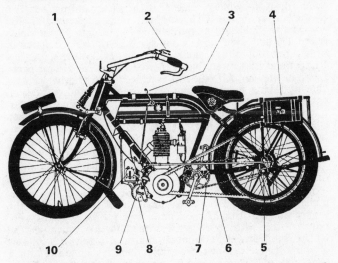

A typical straightforward design of 1910, the 3½ h.p. single cylinder BSA

1. Spring fork with cycle-type brakes
2. Controls all now handlebar mounted
3. Hand and foot gear control
4. Pannier toolboxes and carrier
5. Two-speed hub gearbox
6. Belt drive from engine pulley
7. Pedals and chain, principally for starting
8. Pepperpot silencer
9. Forward-mounted footrests
10. Magneto in front of engine

6. THE VINTAGE ERA 1915-1930

It has been said that there is nothing like a war for advancing research and design, and the motorcycle of 1920 certainly showed very considerable improvements over the corresponding 1915 designs even though production for civilian use ceased in November 1916. Output for war purposes was of course, stepped up and the factories were never so busy; the bulk of the Army requirements was met by Triumphs, who turned out over thirty thousand units during the course of hostilities, nearly all of them fitted with the new Sturmey-Archer three-speed countershaft gearbox and belt drive. The reliability of the machines brought the universal nickname of 'Trusty'. Douglas, too, made considerable numbers of their lightweight two-speed flat twins, all finished in khaki paint (plate 22). In the early days, when a war of movement was expected, orders were placed with Clyno, Royal Enfield and Scott for twin-cylinder sidecar machine-gun outfits, but few of these were made. RAF contracts were allotted to Phelon and Moore, Sunbeam manufactured for foreign governments (plate 17) and even turned out some belt-drive machines to order, but doubtless against their better instincts. A few Rudges and BSAs were also exported for use in distant parts. Later in the war Alfred Scott produced a three-wheeler capable of taking machine-guns over rough ground; it was an extremely practical vehicle although its appearance was distinctly odd—something like a sidecar outfit enclosed in a dish-cover with a radiator in front. He was not awarded any contract, but the factory developed the idea later for civilian use as the 'Scott Sociable', known more familiarly as the 'Crab'.

Some months after the armistice the industry was permitted to revert to civilian production, and the results of wartime thoughts about design became evident. Demand was enormous and prices soared accordingly until such time as the supply situation caught up. One or two pre-war designs were reintroduced with more or less modification, such as the Rudge, the lightweight Triumph and the Norton with its now old-fashioned direct-belt drive and their fast engines with a guarantee of 70 or 75 m.p.h. Apart from the few diehards, direct drive was no more, nor were there any such things in the shops as chain-and-pedal starting or hub gears. The industry had at last realised that there was an essential need for a three-speed countershaft gearbox mounted behind the engine, and nearly all machines were fitted with a multiplate clutch and kickstarter. By 1923 all the larger machines were

22

turning over to all-chain drive, and sidecar outfits at least had dynamo electric lighting. Frames were lower and the top tube was inclined or curved to provide a lower saddle position and enable the average rider to put both feet on the ground. Brakes improved and the era of the internal expanding brake design was but a year or two away; tyres also improved greatly and the safer wired pattern began to supplant the old beaded-edge type which was inclined to jam the wheel dangerously when punctured.

The ultimate development of acetylene lighting was attained about 1930; there was a large choice of makes.

The pent-up enthusiasm of the war years and the soaring demand had tempted many people to enter the industry in a small way and innumerable brand names came on the market, mostly to wither and vanish within a year or two. There was a boom in cheap scooters and in very lightly built cyclecars, some of them with wooden frames, but by about 1922 they were all gone, the sound and experienced Morgan design alone being left to continue for another twenty years.

The motorcycle itself was now a thoroughly practical affair, able to go anywhere in the world with comfort, speed and economy, and the variety and quality of British machines available for touring or racing were unmatched in any other country then or since. All forms of motorcycle sport throve, long and historic tours were undertaken throughout the five continents and records were broken regularly. Literally dozens of firms created competition departments and strove to carry off honours at national and international races, and rivalry was so keen that almost every race could be won by any one of the entrants. Enthusiasm and sportsmanship mattered in the main more than pot-hunting, and a racing club-man would have laughed to scorn the idea of taking his ma-

23

chine to meetings in a van: motorcycles, even racers, were after all for riding.

Year by year improvements were made in the hopes of stealing a march over one's rivals; design was fluid and there were plenty of differences of opinion about the best features of an efficient motorcycle. One saw an immense variety of machines on the road or at club meetings, and the comparisons and arguments were endless. Roads were uncluttered by very many cars—the 'blue, empty roads of Britain' they were called by Lawrence of Arabia, and almost everyone you met was a fellow enthusiast.

This was the day of the businessman-devotee who founded his own firm, designed, built, rode and raced his own products, and sold them to the public. This had already been done, of course, by A. A. Scott, James Norton, the Collier and Stevens brothers, but the scope was now wider. Jock Porter won the 1923 Lightweight and 1924 Ultralightweight TT and went into production with his machine, the New Gerrard, in Edinburgh. Howard R. Davies, having won the Senior TT in 1921 on a 350c.c. AJS, considered he could design something better, and proceeded to win the 1925 Senior on a machine of his own make, the HRD. This was put on the market, proved a success, and was later fitted with the Vincent spring frame. As the Vincent-HRD, it became one of the most famous of all post-Second World War machines.

George Brough was perhaps the doyen of them all. Dissatisfied with existing designs in 1919, he built his own big twin racing solo, and with it took fifty-one fastest times at fifty-one meetings (plate 19). The fifty-second brought disaster when a tyre came off, so he turned his attention to producing machines to order, first in the factory of his father, W. E. Brough, and later, as the Brough Superior, on his own (plates 25 and 29). His flair for publicity led him to design a tank shape so distinctive that his machines were instantly recognisable and the appearance continued very little altered until the last were built in 1940; the saddle-tank was probably his invention. The machines were made to personal measurement and were expensive, and Brough earned his reputation as the maker of the 'Rolls-Royce of motorcycles' (plate 21). It was rarely that the autumn show did not provide a sensation by way of something very unorthodox from the Nottingham factory. 'G.B.' himself entered regularly for all British and European long-distance trials and was at one time the fastest man on two wheels.

There were so many other practical racing men that it seems invidious to give further examples, but the merits of two more at least demand a mention: C. G. Pullin, winner of the

1. *Typical of the tricycle designs which flourished at the end of the nineteenth century is this Deschamps of 1898, built very much along de Dion lines. Note the spoon brake working on the front tyre.*

2. *The Werner machine of 1899. Rated at a nominal 1½ h.p., it was the first motor bicycle to sell in Great Britain in any quantity and had several imitators.*

3. *The first Singer; the remarkable motor-wheel produced in the summer of 1900 by Perks and Birch of Coventry. The engine was a nominal 2 h.p., and this was the first to be fitted with a magneto and a throttle control.*

4. *A Humber of 1902. This employed chain drive and the Phelon and Moore system of sloping engine built into the frame. Several good specimens survive.*

5. The 2½ h.p. Triumph of 1904, fitted with their own engine, an automatic inlet valve pattern already outdated by the Minerva engine they rejected.

6. The remains of an ASL of 1909, with JAP engine and two-speed Albion gearbox. The initials stood for Air Springs Ltd. and the design provided for pneumatic springing front and rear. This was not a success owing to rapid wear of the rubber glands.

7. *The first of the two-stroke lightweights: the 211c.c. Levis of 1911, with direct-belt drive, efficient front springing and no pedals.*

8. *A 1913 Wilkinson, a very advanced design made by the sword people and featuring a four-cylinder water-cooled engine, shaft drive and armchair seating.*

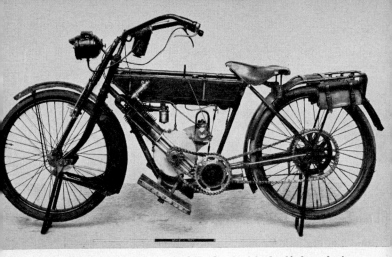

9. *The Phelon and Moore of 1911, fitted with the 3½ h.p. sloping engine. The two primary drives to a counter-shaft with selecting clutch to give two-speed gears can be clearly seen, also the external contracting rear brake.*

10. *Famous machines of all time: 'Old Miracle', the 1912 direct-belt drive sidevalve Norton on which D. R. O'Donovan beat 112 world speed records between 1912 and 1920, including the flying kilometer at 82.85 m.p.h. in 1915.*

11. *This Rex of 1912, with 3½ h.p. sidevalve engine, was equipped with hub gear and rearward mounted magneto. The saddle was particularly well sprung.*

12. *To discover a machine in this state needs a little luck. A 1913 Lea Francis with 400c.c. twin JAP engine, fully enclosed chains, two-speed gearbox with hand and foot clutch, and low-pressure tyres, in 'as found' condition.*

13. *A brand-new Triumph with its proud owner and passenger, taken about 1913. Note the hub gear and contemporary basketwork sidecar.*

14. *The famous Rudge Multi of 1914. This is a single-cylinder example, one of the largest such engines ever made, of 750c.c. Starting by chain and pedals was accomplished with the machine on the stand.*

15. *A 1914 532c.c. Scott restored to its original condition by D. Cox. This design was produced, with minor modifications, for over twenty years. It involved two primary chains with a selecting clutch to give a two-speed gear.*

16. *The Indian, from the USA, with 680c.c. twin engine, front and rear leaf springing, two-speed gearbox and foot clutch. This example dates from about 1915.*

17. *The Sunbeam. This is a 1915-16 model in original wartime livery, as made for export to the Allied armies. It has a 492c.c. engine and all-enclosed primary and rear chain drives.*

18. *A pre-war design successfully reintroduced in 1919. The 'LW' or 'Baby' Triumph of 225c.c. with two-speed gearbox. This particular example has some pre-war parts, presumably found on the shelf when civilian production recommenced.*

19. *Famous machines of all time: 'Old Bill', the big V-twin designed and built for his own use in 1919 by George Brough. It gained 51 fastest times out of 51 meetings and set the pattern for all subsequent Brough Superior designs.*

20. *The works racing Scott sidecar outfit of 1923. On it H. Langman gained the fastest lap in the Isle of Man TT of that year. The outfit can usually be seen at Stanford Hall.*

21. *The 1924 sidevalve flat twin marketed by W. E. Brough, with Sturmey-Archer gearbox, hand-pump oiling and contemporary sidecar.*

22. *Early Douglas owners are lucky in that the year of manufacture was usually engraved on the chain cover. This example dates from 1924, the last year of belt drive. The design was basically unchanged for ten years. The gearbox gives two speeds.*

23. 'Satanella', the 1924-25 790c.c. twin-cylinder AJS on which Lt-Cdr. Oswald Frewin carried out a series of incredible long-distance tours from the Arctic circle to Morocco. The picture was taken in Algeria in 1926.

24. The 1925 500c.c. two-stroke Dunelt, probably the largest of its type ever marketed. It was fitted with a detachable aluminium cylinder head and quick detachable interchangeable wheels. This example is under trade plates.

25. *George Brough at the 1968 Brough Superior Rally at Stanford Hall. The machine is a 1926 SS 100 model with 996c.c JAP engine, capable of a hundred miles an hour.*

26. *First of the redesigned Ariel range: the two-port 497c.c. model of 1927, offered at £50 and claimed to be capable of 90 m.p.h. 'when specially tuned'. Saddle-tanks became the fashion.*

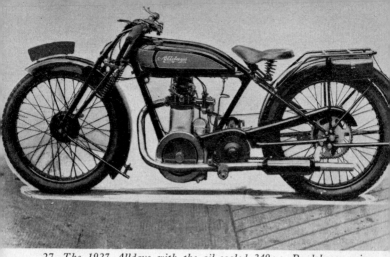

27. *The 1927 Alldays with the oil-cooled 349c.c. Bradshaw engine and a tank finished in royal blue. Most primary chain drives were still exposed at this time.*

28. *Famous machines of all time: 'Old Faithful', the 1928 588c.c. Norton bought new by John Masterman and on which he continues to tour in three continents. His opinions on maintenance are as effective as they are unorthodox. The 'most travelled machine in the world' has over three-quarters of a million miles to its credit—all entirely solo.*

29. *An 800c.c Austin-engined Brough Superior of 1931. Fitted with self starter, reverse gear and shaft drive taken between twin rear wheels. About a dozen were made.*

30. *The 1936 Excelsior 'Manxman' of 350c.c., based on the OHC TT-winning design, was a particularly well-loved model. This example is in racing trim.*

31. *The Royal Enfield 350c.c. 'Bullet' of 1950 with front and rear hydraulic springing and foot gear change. Saddles were still fitted.*

32. *A sectioned example of the magnificent Vincent 1,000c.c. engine of 1951. Its performance could not be matched at the time but its adherents had to defend it against the accusation that it was a 'solution going round looking for a problem.'*

Senior TT in 1914, designed and marketed the Pullin-Groom in 1920 and the Ascott-Pullin in 1928, both luxury all-enclosed machines much before their time; and F. W. Dixon who won the 1923 Sidecar and 1927 Junior races and who completely redesigned the then old-fashioned Douglas range in 1926. Other designers of undoubted genius in the motor-cycle sphere included H. R. Ricardo, remembered for his 1921 four-valve Triumph design, and Granville Bradshaw, an engineer of particularly advanced ideas, responsible among many other things for the Sopwith-built transverse twin ABC, the oil-cooled overhead valve Bradshaw engines (plate 27) and the transversely mounted V-twin Panthette. His designs received universal respect due to their original approach but are said to have required skilled attention to keep them in good running order, and they were rarely competitive in a commercial sense. Barr and Stroud, two Leeds University professors, left their appointments to found a firm for the manufacture of single-sleeve valve engines. Designs of this kind involve a thin steel sleeve with holes cut in it to register with the ports and which moves between piston and cylinder. The engines had many endearing characteristics of smoothness and silence and were fitted by quite a number of firms in the middle twenties, but they did have the disadvantage that any lubrication failure destroyed the engine. The professors later turned their attention to optical instruments.

Valentine Page redesigned the Ariel range with saddle-tanks and new engines in 1927 and gave the old-fashioned firm a thoroughly modern image (plate 26). An American, C. A. Neracher, marketed a revolutionary layout which he called the Ner-a-Car, in 1920. It had a low, open frame, hub-centre steering like the front wheel of the contemporary cars, and a variable friction drive by way of transmission. Represented as proof against skidding, it was irreverently known as the motor-assisted mudguard.

In America, C. B. Franklin redesigned the Indian (plate 16), which had quite a vogue in this country in the early twenties. J. V. Pugh produced a new range of Rudge-Whitworth machines with four valves, four-speed gearboxes and coupled brakes in 1925. Proprietary engines led the way in motive-power design for a while, JAP, Anzani, Precision and Blackburne all offering thoroughly satisfactory high-performance overhead-valve engines very soon after the end of hostilities. Overhead camshafts for valve operation were first introduced by JAP in 1922, to be followed by Velocette in 1924, AJS (a chain-driven design to which they remained faithful for thirty years—plate 23), Norton (plate 28), Calthorpe, Humber and others all round about 1928.

Villiers came out with a magneto incorporated in the fly-wheel—a cheap and compact design for utility lightweights, and good enough to drive all its competitors off the market. Most firms fitted it although Dunelt favoured a two-diameter 'top hat'-shaped piston in their two-strokes, which gave an extra measure of pumping compression (plate 24).

British design was in a state of the utmost vigour. Some few of the varieties available to buyers have been mentioned but it seems almost invidious to single them out among so many. A few minutes with a motorcycle magazine of the twenties will give a better impression of the range then offered. Examples of most of them remain, however, and the discoverer must seek them out for himself.

Ignition intensifiers are as old as sparking-plugs. This is the 'Phaulax', sold by Gamages in 1903 at 1s. 6d. Note the other motoring accessories—ladies' motor veils, foot muffs, motor baskets and paraffin lamps.

7. POST VINTAGE 1931-1945

The early thirties found the industry slowly recovering from a state of depression and many of the famous names as old as motorcycling itself vanished for ever about this time, among them Humber, BAT, Quadrant, Alldays, Raleigh and Rex. Other firms tried hard to attract the poverty-stricken market with changes in design or extra-cheap models, and the spate of new ideas continued unchecked. Reliability was taken for granted, comfort and weather protection received some attention; new spring-frame designs were evolved by Bentley and Draper for the Brough Superior, by OEC, Vincent, New Imperial and others. Royal Enfield, Francis Barnett, New Hudson and Triumph offered all-enclosed machines but the vogue for these seemed to pass rather rapidly and the essential conservatism of the average motorcyclist became evident. The BSA 'Sloper' had already provided greatly improved standards of tractability, silence and easy starting at the expense of a certain degree of performance, but its popularity was probably enhanced by its conventional appearance. Other firms copied it, but only to the extent of supporting a fashion for forward-sloping cylinders. Matchless also had thoughts about refinement and offered the 'Silver Arrow', a monoblock spring-frame V-twin of 400c.c. which deserved more popularity than it received; probably it was overshadowed by the same company's 'Silver Hawk', produced a year later in 1931, a narrow-angle V-four of considerable performance and which earned much praise although it did not last long on the market.

Better luck was experienced by the four-cylinder Ariel, also a 1931 introduction, which employed the more elaborate layout of two crankshafts geared together. In the early models it encountered cooling and distortion problems, cured later by increasing the engine capacity. It was produced for twenty years. Brough produced an in-line water-cooled four-cylinder with an engine by Austin and shaft drive operating between twin rear wheels, but this was strictly for sidecar use and was found to have comparatively little advantage in practice over the orthodox V-twin units. The first Triumph vertical twin (1934) and the first Douglas transverse flat twin (1935) were both commercial failures although some of those who could afford them continued to buy the German BMW, of very similar design to the latter. The redesigned Triumph (1936) was an unqualified success and set one of the main trends for post-war fashion.

By 1930 all machines were being finished in chromium plate,

and electric dynamo lighting was universally obtainable, usually at extra cost; electric horns came a year or two later and have shown no improvement since. A speedometer was always an 'extra' but on the other hand one could rely on being supplied with a good kit of tools and a tyre pump. There was a vogue for high-level exhaust pipes and two-port engines which increased weight more than efficiency. The influence of racing was felt in the general adoption of positive-stop four-speed foot-change gearboxes; again, this may have been fashion to start with, but for most people it was a distinct improvement also. There was a proliferation of dazzling colours about 1930 unseen again until the late fifties, and unlike then, of mercifully short duration. Velocette, Rudge and Sunbeam stuck to the gold-lined black throughout and the playboys soon came back into line when the crimson and royal blue got chipped and rusty after the first few months.

Tank-top instrument panels were seen for a few years after about 1932, and many firms fitted rubber-mounted handlebars for a year or two. Straight-pull brake levers replaced the inverted type everywhere.

The big single-cylinder sidevalve engine remained freely available at prices down to £40, and was especially useful for economical sidecar use; the road organisations bought it in thousands. Villiers-engined lightweights in great variety served the needs of the daily rider to work and were exported all over the world at £24-30 a time. Some rather bad machines were occasionally offered to the public, but not for long, and the general quality of the product continued to be dictated by racing policy and the friendly rivalries thus generated. The various competition departments were bands of devoted enthusiasts for whom nothing in the interests of the firm was too hard or too arduous and they often achieved results which could have been got by no method other than sheer single-minded loyalty. The fast but rather old-fashioned Norton under the design guidance of racing man Joe Craig, produced single-cylinder engines of a power until then considered impossible for the internal combustion engine. The Rudge four-valve radial engine had every merit of technical excellence and logged an enviable number of international wins. Velocette, the firm that never made a bad motorcycle, produced racing machines so consistently excellent that their popularity among private entrants exceeded that of all the other makes put together. Sunbeam, AJS and OK Supreme overhead camshaft designs all had most successful years and were always formidable contenders for honours. Excelsior won the lightweight TT with a design straight off the drawing-board and hence nicknamed the 'Mechanical Marvel'. Such an achievement had previously been thought impossible. The specialist twins, Scott and Douglas, were both in financial trouble and tended, to the regret of many, to drop out of racing; it was evident that the general level of design had caught them up and their own engine types were not susceptible to much more development.

It was nevertheless becoming obvious that the effective limits were being approached in the power output of single-cylinder engines and that the future lay in providing more, and smaller, cylinders. The trend was already being led by foreign designs and returning them successes in racing, and it was a sign of the times when AJS (already merged with Matchless), produced some remarkable inclined parallel twin-cylinder racing machines with a formidable potential, the full development of which was killed by the outbreak of war in 1939.

Production of civilian machines ceased on the commencement of hostilities, but most of the larger firms turned out hordes of dull green or khaki motorbikes for the many military activities at home and abroad which demanded them. They were of necessity sturdy and simple in design, usually heavy and without much performance although capable of withstanding abuse and neglect, even in spite of the maintenance facilities which were usually very efficiently organised. Of such machines, the 16H model Norton, M-series BSA and others gave sterling service, but such of the riders as were already experienced motorcylists usually seemed to prefer the lighter and sprightly designs such as the Ariel, the occasional Velocette and particularly the Matchless with its specially designed hydraulic front fork, a fitting which in one form or another was to become practically universal in the years ahead.

Interest in old motorcycles existed right at the start of the post-vintage era and grew slowly through the war years. The emancipation of the motor vehicle as a result of the Act of 1896 was celebrated at that time by a parade from London to Brighton, and a commemorative run along the same route had been held in 1914. This was probably the first veteran event held anywhere. In 1930 the Sunbeam Club held a similar celebration run, open only to motorcycles manufactured before 1915. It proved so popular with both entrants and spectators that it has been held annually ever since, war years excepted. The standard of machine preparation has improved steadily, and the days when rusty relics appeared at the start, and probably broke down soon afterwards, are long gone. Nobody now remembers that the event was once inaccurately referred to by the ribald as the 'Old Crocks' Race'.

The war years meant for many servicemen long periods of waiting in readiness, and it was to enliven the boredom of such occasions that Captain J. J. Hall and a few friends used to spend their leisure time looking for ancient motorcycles wherever they might find them, restoring them and indulging in informal races before writing about their adventures in the specialist press. It was out of the infectious enthusiasm of these people that the vintage movement was later to be born.

8. THE POST-WAR PERIOD 1946-1960

Although what happened in the years immediately following the Second World War may be thought of as very recent history indeed, there are now plenty of keen motorcyclists about who were not born when that history was made, and it seems to some of them almost as remote a period as the age of the Werner; and since the motorcycles made in the 1946–1960 period differed radically in many ways from those available now, many of them have justly become extremely interesting and collectable items.

It is the fate of most man-made objects as they get old, to go through a dangerous period of obsolescence before they enter a second childhood so to speak, and once again become valued as they were when new. It is, of course, the interim years which result in the destruction of most of the things which subsequent generations are apt to find desirable, and which ensure the scarcity and value of whatever remains. Efforts to preserve any notable design which is no longer in production are worthy of support, and collectors specialising in post-war machines are playing a valuable part in helping to preserve our engineering heritage.

There had indeed been a few collectors of old motorcycles between the wars, men such as Ralph Neville of Beeston, who was able to obtain all the nineteenth-century machines he fancied, but they dwelt unknown and unorganised, and perhaps the most important event from our present point of view came after the war with the founding of the Vintage Motor Cycle Club in 1946 by C. E. Allen, BEM, widely known as 'Titch'. He was able to catch and hold the exact mood of the time; the club grew apace, and this had the important effect of slowing down the destruction of worthwhile machinery of historic interest; industrial archaeology received a shot in the arm and became unexpectedly popular. Soon after this time, the Collectors' Club started up to minister to the interest of vintagents in London and elsewhere, and this caught the attention of Lord Montagu, with his motoring background, who commenced organising the Motor Museum at Beaulieu, largest of its kind and a trend-setter for many other motor museums in various places.

As a natural consequence of the war, prices rose rapidly and demand outstripped supply for a while. Many small machines, scooters and cycle motors reached the market to cater for those needing a cheap method of getting to work, and many of the designs were sound and quite long-lived. The Cyclemaster was a notable case, embodying a compact engine built into the rear wheel almost exactly along the lines of the Singer of fifty years before.

Several forward-looking firms realised that motorcycling would probably not be the same again and that designs would either have to be directed at providing the extra comfort and convenience which was now demanded on all sides, or they must make their products useful only for sport of one kind or another, and as an inevitable result, less well fitted for touring or riding to work.

This is possibly where the industry in this country went wrong. Some firms produced luxury machines while luxury seekers bought cars. Sunbeam offered a most interesting design along new lines with an in-line rubber-mounted twin-cylinder engine, shaft drive, and oversize tyres and mudguards. It proved smooth and long-lived. Douglas completely redesigned their flat twins so that the engine was mounted transversely in a wide duplex frame; a most ingenious form of torsion-bar springing front and rear provided excellent comfort and road-holding qualities. Velocette, retaining their well-loved single-cylinder range with the addition of pneumatic springing, produced a most carefully designed small-size transverse twin with water-cooling, full front and rear springing, shaft drive and efficient weather protection. It was silent, economical and had a lively performance. The police found it ideal for general duties and it survived to become the last sidevalve design available on the British market.

Fashion decreed that the majority of the larger machines should be vertical twins; design varied somewhat, but defects such as vibration seemed to be common to most of them and the advantages they had over the equivalent single-cylinder types in sheer speed seemed by many to be outweighed by extra complication and lessened reliability and life. George Brough did not recommence production but his niche in the market was worthily filled by the Vincent, with its black tank and massive appearance. Both cylinders of the big V-twin engine formed part of the frame, wheels were fitted with two brakes each and were interchangeable, all fittings were of stainless steel and the machine bristled with new ideas. It was unbeatable for fast, long-distance touring and there were still for a few more years sufficient diehards prepared to buy it (plate 32).

Ariel recommenced production of a redesigned 1,000c.c.

square four but finally dropped their entire range in favour of an inclined parallel twin two-stroke engine mounted low in a wide duplex frame with fairings and a false tank. This sold in sufficient numbers to keep the firm in business.

Mergers became the fashion, and many respected names disappeared or remained as rather pathetic examples of badge-engineering on tanks which had never come from the old factories. The Government continued to stress the vital nature of exports during this period and as the fifties went by and good progress was made in the American market, it became evident that features demanded across the Atlantic had to be made available here in the cause of 'unified production', whether home riders wanted them or not. The voices of publicity told them that they did, but many riders did not and got out. The industry cared little because it was now through exports alone that they made what little money they did make. The Americans wanted fun-bikes for tearing round the sandy hinterlands among the cacti, and to which they might clip an assortment of eye-catching gadgets; no American would use a motorbike for serious work. So machines on this side became noisier once more, less economical because small sums of money matter less when one has that holiday feeling, less well mudguarded because one doesn't go out for fun in the rain, and with a high, rough performance which one could not legally use to the full on British roads; they were painted in dazzling colours and fitted with obtrusive exhaust systems. They then came into direct competition with Continental and Japanese products which had many advantages in research facilities and wide markets, and were able in many cases to displace them. A few of the old famous names remained but had little or no connection with the teams or factories which originated those names: mergers had seen to that. The British machine produced primarily for the British rider had ceased to exist.

9. CLUBS, MUSEUMS AND LITERATURE

This chapter is intended to summarise the information available to anybody who wishes to start studying or collecting old motorcycles, and it is hoped that it will provide some useful reference material for a few people who already do so. It does not claim to be complete but may provide a starting point.

Clubs

If you have acquired an old motorcycle and put it in running condition, it is to be hoped that you will ride it occasionally, since it is good that these things should have actual use and not become dusty museum specimens. There are clubs which provide plenty of opportunity for local meetings and runs, and if you feel inclined to take part in a long-distance rally, quite a number of these are organised in the summer months. Reliability trials take place, and there are even well-organised and competitive grass-track and short-circuit road races specially arranged for vintage and post-vintage machines. Advice on all such events can be obtained from the **Vintage Motor Cycle Club** (Secretary, Eric Thompson, 28 Glover Road, Pinner, Middlesex), which issues a monthly *Bulletin* containing a variety of interesting articles and notes, an annual membership listing, a machine register and other data. The club is organised into sections, so that local contacts can be made; it also runs a scheme for the purchase and exchange of spare parts.

If you live in the London area, you should join the **Collectors' Club** (founder Joseph Greer; Hon. Sec., W. S. Gibbard, 'Brambleacres', Hornbeam Lane, Sewardstonebury, London, E4 7QT). Meetings are held at the Tallent Hall, Euston, for lectures, slide shows, discussions and for exchanges of spare parts and literature.

The **Sunbeam Club** is the organising body of the Annual London to Brighton Run each March, and maintains a register of veteran motorcycles. There are also several one-make clubs specialising in veteran and vintage machines, notably for the following makes: ABC, Ariel, Brough Superior, Douglas, Rudge, Scott and Vincent; the addresses of the honorary secretaries for the time being can be obtained from J. B. Wiley, British Motorcycle Federation, 225 Coventry Road, Ilford, Essex.

Meetings

In addition to those mentioned, old machines are often on display at most of the steam fairs and traction-engine rallies which have become popular functions in most parts of the country. Space will not allow more than a mention of the many long distance and international rallies such as the Tour of Birmingham, the Windmill Rally and the Tour of Ireland, but an exception may perhaps be made, by way of example, of the Banbury Run, which has been described as the largest free show anywhere of old motorcycles in action. Machines to the number of about 350 start from the Banbury car park and complete a regularity run of up to seventy miles with time checks on the way, and culminating in the ascent of the fearsome Sunrising Hill, a very popular vantage point for spectators. On their return the machines are eligible for a concours competition. Local events of a similar nature but smaller in scale are held in most parts of the country.

Museums

Many city museums have a veteran motorcycle or two on display, but the majority of motor museums deal largely with four-wheelers with a few motorcycles acquired in the cause of completeness. There seem to be only two motorcycle museums as such in the United Kingdom: Stanford Hall, and Murray's Museum.

Stanford Hall, near Rugby is a fine ancestral mansion; the motorcycle museum is located in the large stable block and contains a wide range of historic machines, many of them famous racers, well displayed and for the most part in good running order. Various TT winners are here, including the Norton which won the first series in 1907. The winner of the first race held at Brooklands, the supercharged big twin which holds the perpetual solo and sidecar records at that unforgettable place, George Brough's personal racer 'Old Bill' (plate 19), together with many other unique machines lent from private collections and changed from time to time. The museum is open in the summer months; postcards and literature are available.

Murray's Museum, The Bungalow, Isle of Man, possesses an extraordinary range of interesting machines, about 150 in all, over half of them normally on view, while many of the others are under restoration in well-equipped workshops. It would be difficult to suggest anywhere else in the world where forty-odd veterans could be seen in a single place; a few of the machines have never even been registered. The museum is open from May to September; a range of postcards and an illustrated guide may be bought.

The National Motor Museum, at Beaulieu, Hampshire, is the place usually thought of when the subject of motor museums is mentioned. Its main display is motor-cars, and its reputation for this is justly fostered by the staff. Comparatively few people realise that it also houses one of the best motorcycle collections in the country, including several prototype and 'one-off' machines, all now housed in the gallery of the palatial new premises, which provide greatly improved viewing. Displays include engines and accessories; literature is available, and there is a comprehensive library and photo service.

Good examples of design of all ages are naturally to be seen at the **Science Museum,** South Kensington, London SW7, although compared with the range available to the authorities, the number on view is a little disappointing, and is very rarely changed. All periods from the nineteenth century to the post-war are, however, represented, including some steam designs, a fine collection of sectioned engines and fittings. Booklets and a photo service are available. Open daily throughout the year.

The **Shuttleworth Collection,** Old Warden Aerodrome, Biggleswade, Bedfordshire, is well known for its vintage aircraft, but it has in addition a rapidly growing motorcycle collection including specimens dating back to 1900. An unusually well produced and informative booklet is available on the two-wheelers. Open days are the last Sunday in each month, March to October.

The following is a sample of the other transport and motor museums: **Caister Castle Motor Museum,** near Great Yarmouth, mainly cars, but also contains about twenty motorcycles, some good, some by no means in original or in working order. There is an 1896 Bollée, a de Dion tricycle of 1900 painted in aluminium, and a unique Eagle water-cooled tricar of 1902. One or two of the later machines are fine, the majority of them are post vintage. **Cheddar Motor and Transport Museum,** Somerset, has a good show of motorcycles even though the emphasis is decidedly on cars once again. About twenty machines are to be seen, some of them lent by private owners, so that the exhibits change from time to time. Most of them are vintage and post-vintage in date; they are well kept but the present arrangement of them is crowded and makes proper viewing rather unsatisfactory. Open all the year round.

Specimens may also be seen at the **Belfast Transport Museum,** Witham Street; the **Glasgow Museum of Transport,** 25 Albert Drive; and the **Manx Motor Museum,** Crosby, Isle of Man. The **East Anglia Transport Museum,** Carlton Colville, Lowestoft, deals mainly in tramways, but is implementing plans for a motorcycle section.

As one would expect, municipal museums sometimes have motorcycles on show, particularly in the Midlands. The collection at the **Birmingham Museum of Science and Industry,** Newhall Street, is good, including quite a number of veteran and vintage machines, engines, etc. Postcards and photographs are available: the building is closed on Mondays. At **Coventry,** besides other machines well worth seeing, they have the four-valve Rudge of 1926 on which Stanley Glanfield went round the world, suffering considerable hardships mostly quite unconnected with mechanical failure. The **Museum of Technology for the East Midlands,** Corporation Road, Leicester, has about a dozen machines ranging from 1904 to 1941, many on loan and changed for other examples now and then. The **Transport Department of Liverpool Museums** has a number of vintage machines including the locally made AER, the most noteworthy being perhaps a 1,000c.c. Bradbury of 1912.

Back in London, the **Imperial War Museum** shows paratroopers' folding 'Welbikes' and one or two others; there is a good example of the 1899 Werner at **Gunnersbury Park** and two or three machines, including a 1904 Humber, at **High Barnet** Museum and several more at **Syon House**. Machines may be on view also at **Hull** and **Brighton.**

Literature

Articles on the history of motorcycling are often to be seen in the weekly and monthly press, particularly *Motor Cycle*, *Motor Cycle Sport* and *Veteran and Vintage*. Many small handbooks on care and maintenance were issued by Iliffes and the Temple Press before the war and are worth seeking on second-hand bookstalls. Of the following list, some books are out of print and may be difficult to get, but nearly all those available can be had through Chater and Scott Ltd., 528-530 Chiswick High Road, London W4 5RG.

Always in the Picture, the Velocette story; R. Burgess and J. Clew; 1971.

Early Days in the British Motorcycle Industry; Eric W. Walford; British Cycle and Motorcycle Manufacturers and Traders Union Ltd., not dated.

Historic Racing Motorcycles; John Griffith; Temple Press Books, 1963 (there are also other books by Griffith).

Motorcycle Cavalcade; 'Ixion'; Iliffe, 1951.

Motorcycles (Science Museum Booklet); P. Sumner; Science Museum, 1972.

The Rolls-Royce of Motorcycles; R. H. Clark; Goose and Son, 1964.

Veteran and Vintage Motorcycles; James Sheldon; Batsford, 1961.

The World's Motorcycles, 1894-1963; Erwin Tragatsch; Temple Press Books, 1964.

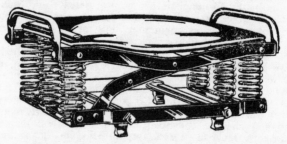

Sprung pillion seats were available from a dozen manufacturers throughout the 1920s. They were regarded as especially suitable for side-saddle riding.

INDEX

53

Some titles available in the 'Discovering' series

Printed by C. I. Thomas & Sons (Haverfordwest) Ltd.,
Press Buildings, Merlins Bridge, Haverfordwest, Pembs.